Five Meanings

A short book about the meaning of life,
why we are here, and how to make the best of it.

ADAM QUIRK

ISBN: 978-1-7365350-0-4

CONTENTS

ACKNOWLEDGMENTS

Dedicated to my parents, Jim and Mary Quirk, for giving me the opportunity to become my best self.

Thank you Brandon Pfeiffer for talking with me about these ideas, and pressing me to explore them further.

Thank you Jane Kupersmith for your editing help and advice.

Thank you Erik Nelson for the cover art, and for being a great sounding board, inspiration, and friend.

Thank you Jessica Quirk for being you. You're honest, caring, loving, creative, and determined. Here's to never half-assing.

"Have fun, learn baseball, do your best."

- Jim Quirk, 1986

INTRODUCTION

A Why-To Book

This is a book about the meaning of life. What follows is an earnest attempt to answer some deep questions that we all face: why we're here, what we're here to do, and how to find meaning in life.

I explain how humanity fits into the big picture of the universe and how the universe created us to be creators.

I look at one human's purpose in the broad landscape of humanity, and why we find deep purpose in creating things for the rest of society to enjoy.

I look at the order of our universe, our society, and our individual abilities, and show how they are naturally linked.

I answer some big questions:

```
Why are we here?
What is the meaning of life?
How do I, Adam, fit into all of
this?
```

We've all been to dark places. Sometimes it takes going there to make new discoveries. That's what happened to me, and why you're reading this now. I wrote this because I needed to. At a low point in my life, I couldn't find a good reason for all of this living. So much work. So much joy. So much suffering. Why? To what end?

It goes to show just how much of everything there is, when so much can be so right and so much can be so wrong.

I've been writing for thirty years, with boxes of notebooks tucked away in all corners of my home. But writing this was different. It changed my life. I thought, wrote, and revised for over two years. I did that work for myself, with no intent to publish it. I wanted to answer these questions for myself. At the end, though, I felt the work was worth sharing.

This could be considered a self-help book. Does the world really need another one? There are already thousands of books about how you should live. There seem to be so many, you'd think every person could find a book that was written just for them, with specific instructions for carrying out each day of their life:

"Today is Tuesday, October 22. You will make a decision today about whether to buy a new toothbrush. It's your destiny—go for it. After checking email, you need to review last week's sales numbers with the remote team. Also, your second child will be born at 5:26 p.m., so congratulations on that. Your drawing of a hippo in the margin of your notebook needs some work. It represents your failures."

—*You: A Step-by-Step Guide to Living for Adam Quirk*, by Tony Robbins or someone like that

There are guidebooks that lead the reader through exercises designed to discover their *passion*. There are books on *forming habits* and *breaking habits*. There are business books on starting up, growing up, failing up, and selling out. I have read a lot of them. So, so many.

These books make up a tapestry of very useful ideas, but they all share a common thread—they focus on *how* a person should do things. How to live. What's more, most of them make me feel like I'm not good enough and I need to follow their instructions to get better. They give tips and recipes for living a better life. Cookbooks, basically.

This is not a cookbook. It precedes the question of *how* to do something. It tries to understand *why* we should do anything at all. If an average self-help book is a stroll through town on your lunch break, this one is a month long vision quest in the forest. But it doesn't rely on mysticism, just reasoning. Feel free to read it in a sweat lodge, though. I certainly sweated a lot writing it.

Road Map

In this first part, I'll tell you why it was important for me to think about these things in the first place. And I try to show my work as I find answers to the big questions. I was driven to seriously search for a meaning of life, and I came out the other side with five of them—meanings, not lives. This first part is roughly sawn. Throughout the rest of the book, I carve out the ideas in greater detail, so they're easier to understand.

In the second part, I dive into what I call Root Meaning. I frame human life in the context of the known physical universe. I think of this deepest meaning of life as a backstop against feelings of meaninglessness we might encounter in times of struggle and pain.

In the third part, I address how we find meaning in our own lives, with other people: Human Meaning. Here I describe a practical approach to meaningful living. It is how I find meaning in everyday life, throughout the week. Human Meaning is found through creating value for your group. Whether that's family, friends, your town, or the whole world, you need them to find meaning. You need your group.

—

Why I Wrote This

The meaning of life. Those words are all pretty simple. Short and easy to say out loud. The only tough one is *meaning*, because it isn't very well defined, or at least nobody can agree on it.

Here are a few of the top competing theories of how philosophers think we should define *meaning*.

- Correspondence theory
- Coherence theory
- Constructivist theory
- Consensus theory
- Pragmatic theory

If you want a discussion of those ideas, you'll need to find another book. I don't fully understand any of them. Abstract theory is the realm of philosophers, and there is value in that work. But for most people, it is too difficult to relate abstract philosophy to your own life.

I try my best not to use too much of the language of philosophy. That field has very specific words that most people don't understand. My goal for writing this is not to break new philosophical ground. My goal is to expose my fellow humans to some ideas that may help them live a better life.

If you do notice me using big words, it probably means I don't really understand what I'm talking about. I'm trying to sound smart by using ten-dollar words where a nickel would do the trick, and you can ignore that particular word deposit. Intelligibility is the ubiquitous aspiration of communicants. See?

To be honest and clear, though, I did not write this with the intention of helping you find *your* meaning. I wrote to discover my own. It became necessary for me to do this after a difficult time in my life. The process of thinking about and writing this book has changed my life for the better.

"The secret to life is meaningless unless you discover it yourself."

—W. Somerset Maugham, *Of Human Bondage*

The hardest work that you'll do in your life is trying to find your own meaning. It's so much easier to do everyday things that seem more *urgent*, like answering email. Important things that are *not urgent*, like thinking about the meaning of life, are really difficult to do. The little things are easy because we know how to do them. We know we can accomplish the task. Thinking about the meaning of life is hard, because we don't know if it's worth the effort.

I'm here to tell you that it most definitely is. This kind of quest can raise you to your highest potential. Because once you know *why*, the *whats* and *hows* are made clear. Purposeful work is one of the most fulfilling things you can do in life. If you know *why* you're making something, you'll have a stronger foundation to build it on.

Most people do want to find meaning but don't have any idea where to start. So instead, they fill their time away from work with distractions. We all use them. Media, socializing, and alcohol—the holy trinity of the American weekend. These things aren't bad on their own. In fact, they can be very good and useful. But if you constantly dull away the sharp edges of life with leisure activities and entertainment, you may not find the time or confidence to tackle your own meaning. The path to your deepest meaning is blazed through the struggle of figuring out your purpose.

I hope that the work I've done to figure out my own purpose can help you to figure out yours.

§

The Starting Point

I am a human man, a husband, a father, a son, a friend, a business founder, and a bunch of other things. In 2018, I was having a hard time being all these things at once. I could manage one at a time, but when they overlapped, I struggled. I was especially tormented by my business during the last half of 2018, to the point where I was questioning the point of continuing it.

I cofounded a distillery called Cardinal Spirits in 2013, and we had been growing at a rapid clip every year since. With every new layer of growth came new challenges. In 2018, our cash flow was having a hard time keeping up with our top-line growth. Any business owner knows how unsustainable that is.

I was internalizing every failure, whether or not I was the cause. Even if bad luck or some other external cause was to blame, I still felt drained and hurt. This was no way to run a business—or a life. Eventually I reached a breaking point.

As usual in tough situations, I called my dad. I told him that I was really struggling and needed some help. I told him that my business was grinding me down. I repeated a few times, "I need some help."

He was there for me. I knew he would be, because he always was.

We'd had a long talk the last time I was at my childhood home in Evansville, Indiana. Just standing around the kitchen after breakfast, we went deeper than we usually get during the daylight hours with no alcohol involved. I had been digging through some boxes of old photos. My wife, Jessica, was making a family history wall in our house and she wanted some ancestor photos. We didn't have many that went back more than two generations to my grandparents. But I kept finding photos of my dad doing all kinds of fun stuff with my sister and me as kids. The ones with just us were taken by my Mom, and there were a few with all four of us that must have been taken by a passerby. It reminded me that he spent a ton of time with me as a kid. He taught me everything from woodworking to baseball to how to ride a bike. He took us on a lot of fun road trips. I mentioned this to him that morning in the kitchen and thanked him for doing it. It wasn't until then that I realized the sacrifice he made to do that. Maybe *sacrifice* isn't the right word, but it was a conscious decision to spend time with his kids instead of working more or doing anything else.

He said that during my childhood, he had lots of opportunities to advance with the company he worked for, but they all required either more travel or relocating. And he declined every time, because his priority was at home. I think it took me having my own children to realize the weight of that kind of decision.

So that November morning on the phone with him, I knew he could help. He always helped. He was always optimistic, even in the hardest times.

He told me to come up to their house, and we could talk it through. So, Jessica and I packed the kids in the car and drove a couple hours to my parents' place. After getting the kids settled, my dad invited me upstairs, and we stood talking in my parents' bedroom with arms crossed. I stared out the window down onto the rainy street below, and he listened to me unload.

I told him I didn't see any point to my work. I felt completely trapped by my business, which was burning cash and had me personally on the hook for loans. I told him that I felt like we're all just running around trying to win prizes (money, success, love, passing down our genes), but at the end of it, we all die and don't get to keep anything for the effort.

He said that my meaning was in the living room, as he pointed through the carpet to my family downstairs. I nodded in tearful agreement. But inside, I knew that wasn't the ultimate answer for me.

He also said that feeling trapped is not sustainable and that I needed to leave my business. Or at least start planning to leave in some amount of time (a year, maybe two). I knew he was right, and I had tried to think through the options before. But having someone else say it was all right to leave was what I needed to hear.

I realized that there was a light at the end of the tunnel, that *feeling* trapped was not the same as *being* trapped. I felt that I would be able to pull out of this nosedive.

Many hugs later, the next day we were back in the car on our way back to Bloomington. I talked to Jess on the drive about what my dad and I had talked about. It felt bizarre to have been so low hours ago and to now feel like the future was bright again. She helped me think about the great things we had instead of my problems.

Over the next few days, I was able to right my mental ship.

I was going to the distillery every day, working as usual. If anything, I was working harder. I talked to my business partner, Jeff, the week after, and told him that I needed to start thinking about an exit plan. He was understanding. He always is. For the rest of our staff, and the rest of my friends and family, I was poker faced.

I also was able to see my business from a different perspective, once I realized that I wasn't trapped by it. I saw that it was not the looming beast it seemed to be when I was feeling so small next to it. I had come to realize that I had control over that emotion, instead of feeling like my business controlled me.

With a lot of focused planning, hard work,

and good luck, Jeff and I were eventually able to turn our cash flow positive and grow out of that situation. Writing this a couple years later, we're stronger than ever and still growing at a remarkable clip.

But solving that business problem didn't solve all of my own. I felt that something was still left unsettled.

The Deeper Truth

I still knew, deep inside, that I hadn't solved my problem. I was able to get through the storm, but without some serious work, I knew I would run into another one soon. How did I let a business problem almost crush my soul? I felt directionless. I was just staying the course toward an unknown destination.

I decided that I needed to better understand myself and my place in the world. My questions were simple but seemed impossible to answer.

Why are we here?

What is the meaning of life?

How do I, Adam, fit into all of this?

This seemed silly. Unless I have a really terrible memory, I don't think anyone has ever figured these questions out. Monty Python made a movie about the meaning of life, but it wasn't a documentary. So why would I think I could handle these questions? The simple answer is that I had to. I didn't see a good path forward without at least attempting to answer them for myself.

Scientists have uncovered a lot of information about "how" we are here. And there have been widely appreciated philosophical ideas, and widespread ideologies in the form of religions that try to answer the "why" questions. There has been a tremendous amount of thought devoted to trying to understand what happens after life is over. And there is a ton of money and energy spent in pursuit of happiness while we are alive.

In the past several decades, religion and philosophy have drawn less and less attention and esteem from our culture. Religion has had a hard time convincing people of its value, since so much of its history has been shrouded in scientifically improbable or impossible untruths, designed to keep people from questioning its God-given authority. So even for those of us who understand and even admire the underlying teachings of a religion, it becomes difficult to swallow the whole pill. Couple that with the fact that many religious leaders have ulterior motives behind their devotion, and it's no wonder so many of their flock have flown the coop.

So where does that leave those of us who have left the church and have not had the luxury of studying philosophy at a university?

For me, I was left floating through life without an atlas. I still had a strong moral compass, thanks to a loving family and childhood education. But my underlying purpose—my meaning—was unclear.

So, I thought, "Well, I guess I'll try to figure out the meaning of life."

Digging a Foundation

To start, I tried to figure out if I was even asking the right questions. What does *meaning* even mean? I read tons of definitions of the words *meaning* and *purpose*. That led me to read more about language itself and how our brains use language to understand the world. Alexander Stern's work was a great introduction.

Human beings are brazen animals. We have lifted ourselves out of the world —or we think we have—and now gaze back upon it detached, like researchers examining a focus group through one-way glass.

Language is what allows us to entertain this strange, but extraordinarily productive, thought. It is the ladder we use to climb out of the world.

—*Alexander Stern, "The Way Words Mean"*

Later I especially enjoyed reading Douglas Hofstadter's book *Surfaces and Essences*, about how we use analogy to describe everything we experience. This is the opposite of computers, which use digits to build concepts up from bits. We assign meaning to things only by associating them with other things (using "things" here to mean literally everything you can think of, feel, and experience, not just physical objects).

But this path—understanding language better—didn't help me uncover any truths about what we're doing here in the first place.

To be sure I hadn't just missed a really important day in school, I read philosophers to see if anyone had already figured out the meaning of life. My practice was pretty simple. I would think about an idea, Google it, read about it on Wikipedia, then click through to the originator of the idea. Sometimes that would lead me to read essays about the concept. Sometimes it would require me to read an entire book. Wikipedia is an ideal resource for this kind of work, but skipping around it can lead to not fully understanding each piece of the puzzle. So I bookmarked articles, came back, and tried to digest them fully over the course of a week or so. The brain isn't great at understanding big concepts immediately. It needs time for them to intermingle with old ideas, find its own connections and analogies.

I read Epictetus and was drawn to stoicism. But I found that a stoic sees no deeper meaning in life. They live according to natural laws and aim to reach a state of human flourishing or prosperity. But still, what's the point of that?

I read Ben Franklin's autobiography and loved his tactical approach to living a good life. But I couldn't find any deeper reason for doing any of the great things he did.

I read *The Prophet, The Tao of Pooh, Other Minds: A Universe from Nothing, Seven Habits of Highly Effective People*, and *Man's Search for Meaning*, and lots of other summaries of philosophies. They all contributed ideas, but none of them had the synthesis I was looking for.

I listened to podcasts and read dozens of essays on *Aeon.com*. I reread novels and books that had moved me earlier in life. My old friends Steinbeck, Hemingway, and Dickens reminded me of the beauty and pain of human life. And at a meta level, their genius reminded me what we are capable of.

I tried to produce an answer from it all. It's worth pointing out that "producing an answer" is a pretty lofty goal, considering the questions. I cringed at the scale of that goal but needed it as a starting point.

I read and ruminated for the rest of the winter of 2018. In early spring of the following year, I set out to answer these questions for myself. For most of 2019, I wrote. I saw my life and the world in new ways through writing.

I spent months writing and rewriting, chewing on ideas and spitting them out, only to pick them back up again. I turned them over and over in my mind until I could explain them to myself as simply as possible.

The focus for me was reason and purpose, rather than love and emotion. I count myself extremely lucky to have plenty of love in my life. But for me, greedily, I need both. I need to feel good and feel love, but I also need to know my purpose and understand why I'm here. And for whatever reason, I could not feel enough purpose from just loving others and being loved. That was a hard thing to admit to myself, because it seems like love should be enough. I mean, the Beatles said it's all you need.

But as a social creature, I need to feel that society has a purpose so I can feel good serving society. I want to feel that we're building toward something better and that I'm part of that.

To find a deeper meaning, I needed to start

at the very beginning.

I saw that my being alive is directly related to the existence of everything. I can only be alive today because the universe exists with me in it. So, the question of "why am I here?" is directly related to the question "why is *anything* here?".

So why does anything exist? That question led me to read theories of universe formation. If you want to learn about this, I suggest reading *A Universe from Nothing: Why There Is Something Rather Than Nothing* by Lawrence M. Krauss. It gave me a better understanding of how we are here through eons of cosmic evolution. But it got me no closer to *why*.

I began a thought experiment: If I was alone in the universe—completely alone in a dark vacuum—would there be any purpose to my life?

I imagined myself floating in black space. I thought about all of the ways a person can act upon himself, physically, psychologically, emotionally. If you were truly alone, you could still do things. You could think. You could feel and observe reality, although your perception would be limited to what was going on inside the envelope of your own skin. Assuming I didn't need to eat or breathe, and could live in a vacuum, I could change myself by altering my mind through meditation.

I decided that meditating even to the point of nirvana would not be very meaningful, because it would only benefit myself. If there is nothing else going on, why bother attaining "total consciousness," as Carl puts it in *Caddyshack*? Is there inherent value in improving oneself? It seemed to me that you only really find meaning if there is someone (or something) else to receive your value, or at least acknowledge it.

If you run a thought experiment that you're the only person in your town or city, you could keep the landscaping looking nice by mowing the grass. You could repair things when they break, paint things when they peel, and focus on the general upkeep of making things pleasant to live around. Why would you do any of that if there was no one else to appreciate it? Why would you do anything at all?

But then I began thinking about my place in the universe, and what it means to be human within the context of physical reality. I realized that through millions of years of restructuring, the Milky Way had formed, the sun had formed, Earth had formed, and life had evolved to create me, Adam.

I am very much a physical part of the universe that created me. My atoms were forged in the center of stars, which were formed by the laws of physical existence. So, in a very real sense, I am an embodiment of the physical universe in a human form. I'm a fruit of the universe.

It took a tremendous amount of time and energy for the universe to take on this form called Adam. I could feel a responsibility to the rest of the universe to make something of myself for this reason alone.

That was a revelation for me. I was on to something. I felt something akin to power. But I was not satisfied. It only uncovered a new question.

What am I here to do, as this physical, living realization of the universe?

Before answering that, I decided to look at what I *can* do.

First, I have the power of *perception*. I can

perceive my experiences using my senses of sight, hearing, taste, smell, and touch. Plus, I can accentuate those natural senses through tools of detection like telescopes and microscopes. I can observe and experience the universe. In this context, I am the universe looking into a mirror and observing itself, and I'm also the mirror.

Second, I can contemplate my experiences and develop new meanings from them. I can remix ideas in novel ways and develop new understandings of my world. I can try to make sense of it all through analogy and reasoning.

Third, I have the power of creativity. I can alter myself and my environment through mental and physical work. Change is inevitable in the universe, and nothing is static. In this sense, I am the universe recycling parts of itself and rebuilding itself.

Fourth, I have the power to choose my own actions. I can wield my power of observation by choosing where to look. I can wield the power of creativity by choosing what to build. In this context, I am the universe directing its own evolution.

This fourth power was the most important

realization for me.

Before us, the universe did not seem to have *agency* (the capacity to act independently and to make choices) but was determined by its own structure. The laws of physics and nature dictated the course of time and space and all of its inanimate and living inhabitants.

With the human mind, the universe has built itself a new method of evolution. As the agents of the universe, we *choose* how we perceive, discover, and change our world. We call the shots. And we may very well be the only decision-makers in the universe, if you believe the Fermi paradox. And even if we're not alone, we're the only ones in this neighborhood.

We are conscious members of a physical universe, and we are purposefully altering that universe. We are made up of parts of the universe that have formed into human minds in order to further the cause of the universe. In this context, "the brain of the universe" is a good metaphor for humanity.

So, we decide how to perceive, understand, and change our world and are built handily for all of these tasks.

Throughout nature, unique natural-born gifts are exploited by all species. With that in mind, our "natural" purpose would be guided by what we are built for. As the brains of the universe, our role is to decide, to look, to think, and to create. We are here to change our world, and we are uniquely suited to do so.

In other words, **we should do what we are good at, because that is what we are made for.**

The answer to "what should I do as this living embodiment of the universe" seems to be "do what humans are made to do."

That leads to another consideration. If our species is logically supposed to do what humans are good at, maybe each of us should do what we're individually good at too. If each of us is a new arrangement of the universe in a unique form, then we should each be aware of that uniqueness and even try to maximize our uniqueness. Maybe I should just be myself without much worry about conforming to social norms. Maybe I should work to be the most *me-like* I can be. Maybe I should develop my unique talents as far as I can take them. If that principle holds true through other aspects of life, it colors all kinds of decisions. It could be used to decide what each of us should choose to do for a career or what kind of company or product or art to create.

This train of thought led me to understand a deeper meaning behind my natural self-improvement motivation.

Personal development is rooted in a natural drive to be the most me-like I can be.

But I still was missing something important.

If I run the thought experiment of being alone in the universe again, I'm left feeling empty, even after improving myself to the point of ultimate Adam-ness. I seem to need something else in order to find meaning. Because what good are my unique perspective, skills, and creations if there is no one else to benefit from them? Self-development is ultimately not meaningful if I can't share the fruits of that development back to at least one other person.

This seems to be a fundamental truth:

meaning and purpose are impossible in a vacuum. To say that a colder way: an individual agent has no purpose unless it interacts with a system. This is as true in nature and physics as it is in human society. No single thing has any inherent purpose, but observed as part of a system, every single thing serves a purpose.

So, I am here to be my unique self, to discover and change the world around me based on my unique perspective and abilities, and to share those discoveries and creations with my fellow humans (my "system").

In this way, I can choose how I grow and change, and my growth and change benefit the system, which in turn is also growing and changing. Because as agents of the universe, and a system of agents at that, our job is to be the "deciders" and choose what to change.

$\S$

When I first began thinking about this, I was frustrated by the complexity of finding my place within the cosmos and human society. But after talking through these ideas and breaking each one into smaller, more manageable parts, I could provide for myself a decent atlas for living.

Once you make your peace with the big picture (you're part of the universe), you can focus on smaller parts of the picture (you're a unique person), and feel good about making progress in your own direction, for a larger purpose (the rest of humanity).

You can understand how your unique brushstroke will affect the larger painting. You can feel confident that your point of view adds valuable perspective to the problems you solve with others. You can find meaning as a single, important block in the grand Jenga tower of the universe.

After all of this writing, I was able to summarize what I had come to believe as true:

1. You are the universe trying to understand and change itself.

2. You should do what you are made to do: observe, understand, decide, create.

3. Deciding is our most valuable ability, because we are the only ones who can do it.

4. You should evolve yourself into the most uniquely *you* version possible.

5. Share the abilities you develop with the world to find deeper meaning.

I went searching for *the* meaning of life and found five of them. I found why we are here in the universe and how a human can live a meaningful life among other humans. The rest of the book explores these in detail.

MEANING ONE:

You are the universe.

"We have been looking to Nature for an understanding of the big concepts since the dawn of time. We must consider (house) foundations in the light of many varied requirements. The primary job of any foundation is to support the structure above by transferring all loads and forces to the ground. Most plants and animals accomplish this by getting wider at the base."

— *John Connell, Homing Instinct*

What is the widest thing you can think of?

You need a very broad foundation if you want to support all of the activities of humanity, and what is broader than the entire universe? The first meaning, *You Are the Universe*, is the underlying support structure of all other meanings we may find in life. I like thinking of it as my "root meaning" or "foundational meaning." Without it, the weight of human meaning and your individual meaning is unstable.

Root meaning lies beneath the meaning you may find from living a life dedicated to your family or to your work, or experiencing a beautiful sunrise in the mountains. This deeper meaning is what allows you to enjoy those other ways of finding meaning. Because without a deep foundation of meaning based on understanding our role in the universe, those other meanings may not seem to serve any larger purpose. That wouldn't *make* our lives meaningless, but it allows us to consider the possibility.

What does it mean to be human in the broad context of the universe?

Put simply, root meaning is that we're each physically a part of the universe. We are made up of stuff that existed on our planet, which was formed from parts of the universe. We are born *from* the universe, not born *into* the universe from somewhere else. We bud out from the tree of life as fruits of the universe. How in the hell did we do that?

$\mathcal{S}$

In the Beginning ...

What we know about the cosmos has grown substantially since I first learned about its origins in Catholic school in the 1980s. But actually, we still don't know what happened in the very beginning. It seems there was not actually a large bang. The entire universe first came into existence as a small but incredibly energetic ball of ... stuff.

The Big Bang was not really an explosion in space, because before it, there was no space to explode into. Instead, it was the sudden appearance of space everywhere in our dimension (the birth of the universe). It started as a very hot, very dense single point of space about 13.7 billion years ago. After it was born, it grew up very fast. In the period known as inflation, our universe doubled in size about ninety times in less than a second. After inflation, the universe grew at a slower rate, and matter formed.

Matter forming was pretty important, because that's what we're made of. The building blocks of our bodies, our books, our cheese wheels, everything we like.

A few hundred million years after the Big Bang, clumps of matter (gases) began to collapse into each other and form the first stars and galaxies. In our neck of the woods, our sun was formed about nine billion years later. So, we're pretty late to the party, at only 4.6 billion years old.

That is what physics can teach us about our origins: first there was a rapid spread of matter, then a cooling of matter, then a merging of matter. The Earth and all of its future inhabitants were part of that. Earth formed in a lovely little neighborhood called the Goldilocks Zone, where the heat from the sun is just warm enough to support life on the surface. That's where we come in.

It took a while to cool down from a ball of molten rock into a solid object. From the period of boiling-hot magma-covered Earth with zero life to cooled-down Earth with oceans full of single-celled life took about 800 million years.

Then the party really gets started. Single cells start hanging out with other single cells. They realize they can live better lives by working together. Eventually they realize they might as well just stick together for the duration of their life, and multicellular organisms are born.

From there, evolution goes nuts, and the kingdoms of plants and animals spring forth. Five hundred million years ago, vertebrates appear. Six million years ago, humans diverge from our ape mothers. Five hundred years ago, we started printing books. About sixty years ago, we start firing ourselves off into space, and soon after fire emails off to our friends.

The speed at which we have developed from simple worms into feeling, conscious agents of the universe is mind-bogglingly fast or slow, depending on your perspective.

In this context, it's easy to trace our lineage all the way back to the beginning of time and space. We can begin to grasp the grandeur of our existence by seeing ourselves as indivisible from this universal system. It took a tremendous amount of time and energy to build brains that are powerful enough to allow us to understand this stuff.

All of this time and energy just to make me? I, for one, feel a responsibility to the rest of the universe to make something of myself!

This realization, that we are a living

evolution of the universe, supports all the other possible meanings in life. It lifts them up to a higher purpose. When you're ready to give up on humanity, and your own life doesn't seem worth a damn, this Root Meaning is the logical reason to keep on truckin'. It's impersonal but powerful. If you can remember that you are the universe—that you are literally an agent and aide of the universe—it gives you a sense of power and control that is difficult to find anywhere else.

And the real fun hasn't even started yet. Next let's look at how uniquely suited we are to be the agents of the universe.

MEANING TWO:
Do what you are made to do.

So, here we are, integral members of the structure of the universe. In that way, we are just like all the other matter and energy in the Universe. I interact with gravity in the same way as an equally heavy bag of rocks. But we are also distinct from the rest of the Universe. Come, let's marvel together at our wonderful abilities.

As a human, you have certain gifts that other members of our universe do not. Primarily, the ability to choose what to do. Below that primary difference lie a few other important talents. You can perceive and understand the world. You can create change. And you can wield these powers on yourself, and on everything else. Let's think about how, and more importantly, *why* we do this.

It's time to unwrap our gifts.

Observation

First off, we're really good at observing. You can perceive the world around you, which as far as we know is common among all forms of life. Even a single cell has some methods of perception. Some microbes can detect changes in light, temperature, and chemicals. These are methods of perception that we share across the entirety of life on Earth. So we should not feel special for being able to see a predator's shape or hear its growl. Plenty of animals can smell the roses.

Different types of life are better at different methods of perception. Humans rely heavily on five main methods: sight, sound, smell, taste, and touch. But our versions of these senses are not the same as other life forms. For instance, we don't see UV light as well as butterflies can. We don't hear high frequencies as well as dolphins or bats do. We don't smell as well as dogs can. We rely on a limited spectrum of available information to "see" our world.

So, what makes humans so special at observation? Tools. We create and use tools to boost our perception. Tools allow us to observe phenomena that are invisible to any other creature on Earth. We can see into the farthest reaches of space with telescopes. With microscopes, we can observe objects that are smaller than the smallest microbe, down to the elemental building blocks of matter. With data tools, we can uncover invisible patterns. We have increased our own powers of perception so we can explore and observe anything we want. From the first stone tools to the Large Hadron Collider took about 2.5 million years. Just a blink of the eye in cosmic time.

Understanding

Secondly, we're good at figuring things out.

From all of this focused perception, aided by purposefully designed tools of observation, we begin to *understand* the rose. We see it more deeply, and in greater contexts. We associate it with other plants and find analogies to all sorts of other parts of life. We can use it as an example of things that are red when teaching children their colors. We can use its upright habit to form beautiful hedges between parts of yards and sidewalks that require visual separation. We can extract the essences of its scent to produce perfumes that help mask other less desirable odors or to attract the olfactory attention of a potential mate. We understand how a rose can be seen as a metaphor for human life that blossoms from a small bud, blooms ecstatically for a period of time, then dies back again, leaving behind only dry petals as memories of once-glorious beauty.

This pathway of curiosity, observation, and understanding has been going on for as long as we have been making tools. It is one of the things that makes us distinctly human.

Our endless curiosity drives our observations deeper and deeper into the fabric of time and space, so that we continually discover more and more about the reality we inhabit. We use this understanding to paint a broader and more detailed landscape of our natural world. And such deep and broad understanding of our world allows us to better know how to act within it and upon it.

In that context, I'm developing a better understanding of the universe by trying to place humanity in the context of the universe. The universe is trying to understand itself by writing this book.

Through seeking deeper understanding of our world, we attain a deeper understanding of *ourselves* and *how we fit* into the universe. As the most intelligent beings on our planet, it's our responsibility to study our world in the deepest and broadest sense possible. And through deeper understanding, we can find meaning.

Changing Things

Third, we're really good at changing things. This is an instinctual drive we share with almost all other life. Even bugs build nests and change their environment to better suit themselves. But humans differ from the rest of life in some important ways. We not only change our environment, we change ourselves and our society.

For years, I battled an idea I could not shake. Many popular philosophies teach to embrace reality as it is, to not desire anything, and to simply be present in the moment. For me, this means to simply *be*. But without desire, nothing can purposefully change. Suffering would continue forever. On a small scale, if you fell down and cut your leg on a rusty nail, would you just have to accept that you will get infected and lose your leg?

On the other hand, if you're constantly

trying to change things for the better, you become frustrated that your desired outcome is not here yet. This is the nature of wanting.

So, I found myself struggling between choosing *to be* or choosing *to do*.

Once again, I found my answer in nature.

Everything is always changing at an atomic level. Nothing is static. Everything you see around you that appears to be stationary (big concrete buildings, the earth below your feet) is in a state of constant change. At a macro level, it is eroding by the forces of weather. At an atomic level, these large, immovable objects are nothing more than trillions upon trillions of particles, swooping this way and that through spacetime, interacting with themselves and each other every millisecond.

If we have sensory organs so that we can perceive the world around us, then we are surely here to observe. But we also have hands, and a brain that is dead set on building things, whether it's a family or city or company or a little vehicle made out of Legos. So, it's obvious we're here to change things too.

Lying on the grass with your eyes closed, completely still, whether you're alive or dead, you're changing. If you're alive (lucky!), you're changing the composition of gases and the temperature in your environment. If you're dead, your decomposing body is putting materials back into the earth via bacteria and insects. And there's no getting around it. Change is the only thing I can think of that is an absolute in every situation, everywhere the universe. So as conscious beings with a genetic drive to change our environment, it's our responsibility to try to harness that curious "change" energy. Not energy in a mystical sense, but in the sense that if change is a waterfall, don't fight against it. Don't try to swim up the waterfall. Just ride over the edge and try to do cool tricks on your way down.

If change is the only true constant, it would be silly to think that we're *not* here to change things. For me, there's a lot of joy to be found in successfully changing things, making things better. From sanding and finishing a piece of wood to building a company that hopefully changes the way people feel. Those are some ways I find meaning. By keeping a balanced mind, I remember to *just be* when I can, and remember to be present even when I'm *doing*.

MEANING THREE:
Deciding is your superpower.

Agents of the Universe

Now for our most important ability. We have choice. We act upon the universe in novel ways. We change things in ways that are outside the capacity of the raw power of the universe itself through basic physical (nuclear, gravity, etc.) activity.

We make choices to guide our observation, understanding, and creativity. Our conscious minds allow us to make decisions about where to look, rather than looking only where instinct pulls us. We perceive what we choose to perceive. While dogs may have a more refined sense of smell, they use it largely for instinct-driven purposes. They may stop and smell the roses, but only to know if they're edible or if another dog has urinated on them.

As humans, we smell roses to remind ourselves of the beauty of life. And importantly, we choose to smell, touch, and look at them closely in order to further understand their complexity. We discover which volatile organic compounds make up their memorable scent. We know what their pollen looks like and how it is used to reproduce. We know how it grows, how it dies, and how best to keep it looking nice in a garden or vase.

With a deep enough understanding of something, be it a rose or a problem, we can create an appropriate solution that maximizes the outcome for the entire system (including our self, humanity, and the rest of the universe).

Consciousness gives us this capacity. Before us, the universe did not seem to have agency (capacity to act independently and to make choices) but was determined by its own structure. Since we came along, the universe has developed this capacity to direct its own future.

The universe: It's big. It's small. It's everything. It's tied together with string. Imagine threads, linking every particle, pebble, and person to each other in infinite combinations. And then was born free will and the choice of every person to yank on the thread of their choosing, pulling closer to one thing, leaving another behind, but always connected, never fully apart.

Anthropocene is the term some scientists use

to describe the era we live in, where human decisions influence most of what we experience on Earth. Common knowledge is that the Anthropocene began sometime around the Industrial Revolution, when we began mining and using fossil fuels. I'd argue that it started when we harnessed the power of fire thousands of years ago.

Regardless of when it began, a human-controlled Earth is largely a positive outcome when viewed from the perspective of the universe becoming conscious. This is becoming a controversial opinion.

We are experiencing growing pains as we learn how to more carefully wield our global influence. But we learn from our mistakes and are well on our way to becoming more beneficent shepherds of the lands we inhabit.

We have chosen to create national parks to preserve raw nature and enjoy their existence beyond the value of visiting them directly. Their sustainable existence is proof we can understand and guide complex natural systems with a gentler human touch.

From a purely human perspective, it would be difficult to debate the value of agency and of living in a human-dominant environment. There are still pockets of wilderness where this is not the case, and humans alive today who were pioneers of land that was previously wild. Most would say modern life is much preferable to the experience of toiling all day for clean water and nutritious food, all while fearing a predator might kill you or your child or that you may catch an infection that ends your life. There are certainly lots of problems with the way we live today, but we're smart enough to solve them all.

SUMMARY OF ROOT MEANINGS

The Difference Between
Purpose and Meaning

Tools are made for specific purposes. You don't use a golf club to eat soup; you use a spoon. The universe has evolved humans to be incredible observers, learners, and creators. That seems to be our purpose.

But for some, including me, clear *purpose* may not be enough to find deeper *meaning*. There is still an itch that needs to be scratched: why should I care to function as a cog in the gearing of the universe, even if my species is the perfect cog?

It led me to ask the question, *what is the difference between purpose and meaning?*

Purpose is the usefulness of something or the underlying reason something exists. The purpose, it seems, of people is to observe and rearrange reality to better suit their *system*, because as I found earlier, an individual without a system is purposeless. So if purpose is external, or at least interdependent on the system we live in, what does that mean for our individual meaning?

If we are just here to optimize the system,

what is the point? Who are we creating value for? Is it all for us humans? Do we serve all of the animate and inanimate objects in reality? If we are just here to benefit a larger system, is the system self-aware enough to be grateful for our toil? Or are we toiling away at optimizing a system that doesn't care to be optimized because it has no awareness?

Are we possibly here as individual human agents to optimize our system to the point that the system itself gains awareness, as a global and eventually universal conscious being? That's a wild assumption. But even running with that idea, how do we understand intention? Is the system like a bee colony, in that no one individual is directing the show, but every actor knows their part anyway? Then, is there a destiny for the system— something like an optimized beehive?

If our value is tied to the system, our individual lives seem insignificant. What's the point?

This line of questioning led me to an understanding of *time* in the context of meaning. So far, I've talked about being human in the present universe and how we got here.

The way we were built and function can be traced back with a straight line to the dawn of time. What we need now is a reason to go forward into the unknown future.

As usual, we can look to nature for this as well.

More Better Options

The universe can be understood by observing the physical laws of nature. But the universe may also be seen as a form of life. The definition of life is fuzzy, and it sure seems that the universe fits a lot of the criteria. It began as a seed (Big Bang), it grew up (Inflation), and it is now entering its adulthood. As the brains of this universal body, the president of the Universal HOA, it is humanity's choice what happens next in our neighborhood.

If you think of the universe itself as a living thing, you can assign some obvious biological traits. Most importantly, a living organism is not ambivalent about its own life. It needs to survive, grow, and reproduce.

As humanity becomes more and more conscious, more networked, so our brains can work together to solve more complex problems, maybe our future is actual universe expansion. What does any living organism want? It wants to thrive in its existing state, but it also wants to reproduce. If the environment is right, it wants to colonize new territory.

Humans could develop a global consciousness: a vastly more powerful intelligence than we have now. We could use that power to colonize the galaxy, possibly other galaxies, possibly other universes, or possibly even create other universes. I'm not recommending this, by the way. But it seems naturally logical.

That would be our universe, using humans, to cause its own reproduction and territory expansion.

We're already doing this now with theoretical physics, by trying to determine the potential for the existence of other universes and dimensions. If we determine them to be possible, we'll surely try to observe them. And if we can observe them, we'll surely try to visit them. It's in our nature.

And as reproductive agents of the universe, we may choose to procreate more universes.

"In the 1980s, the cosmologist Alex Vilenkin at Tufts University in Massachusetts came up with a mechanism through which the laws of quantum mechanics could have generated an inflating universe from a state in which there was no time, no space and no matter. There's an established principle in quantum theory that pairs of particles can spontaneously, momentarily pop out of empty space. Vilenkin took this notion a step further, arguing that quantum rules could also enable a minuscule bubble of space itself to burst into being from nothing, with the impetus to then inflate to astronomical scales. Our cosmos could thus have been burped into being by the laws of physics alone.

The kind of cosmogenesis envisioned by Linde would require physicists to cook up their cosmos in a highly technical laboratory, using a far more powerful cousin of the Large Hadron Collider near Geneva. It would also require a seed particle called a 'monopole' (which is hypothesized to exist by some models of physics, but has yet to be found). The idea goes that if we could impart enough energy to a monopole, it will start to inflate. Rather than growing in size within our Universe, the expanding monopole would bend spacetime within the accelerator to create a tiny wormhole tunnel leading to a separate region of space. From within our lab we would see only the mouth of the wormhole; it would appear to us as a mini black hole, so small as to be utterly harmless. But if we could travel into that wormhole, we would pass through a gateway into a rapidly expanding baby universe that we had created."

-Zeeya Merali for AEON,
"The idea of creating a new universe in the lab is no joke"

And the question I've asked myself, if all those far-fetched predictions come to pass, is it worth doing all that?

Many of us rightly have apprehension

about human expansion throughout the galaxies. We are currently in a bit of a mess on the surface of our home planet due to unconstrained human expansion. So, worrying about the prudence of colonizing the galaxy is valid, because we have screwed some things up here on Earth. That worry is based on current reality.

But handwringing about progress, growth, and expansion is not necessary. As we become a wiser species, we naturally become more benevolent toward our environment. We may decide to set aside "galactic nature preserves" in the future. Who knows? The point is, we have come a long way from slash-and-burn agriculture, through the Inquisition, through industrialization, and have already solved most environmental and societal problems on paper. We've only been digging up oil and coal en masse for a few hundred years. We quickly realized this was not a sustainable form of energy and are making relatively swift changes to our infrastructure to replace them. Imagine how much faster we'll be at course-correction in the future.

The examples of global consciousness and

universe expansion above are not my proposed strategies for our future. They are meant to represent the unknowable options we may create for ourselves through the work of being good humans. We're creative and always find a good way forward.

Humans continually progress toward more powerful intelligence, so we can observe, learn, and change more. Those are prerequisite to a better future that is unknowable but likely is very desirable. The ability to understand and shape our reality seems to be a very desirable outcome—to have higher levels of choice. Progress is a prerequisite for more, better options in the unknowable future.

So how do we get there? That requires contributing back to our system and all sorts of human growth and interconnection. And how do you do that? You live a life that has purpose: by learning, discovering, innovating, creating, teaching. Living with the intention to create a better future is a way to find deep meaning in life.

§

Before we move on, one more question. If

humanity exists to provide the universe with the ability to decide and act upon itself, there's another question to answer before we proceed: Should we assign values of good or bad to our decisions? Desired outcomes versus less desired outcomes? How best should we wield the power of agency?

The best answer I've found for that is that "good vs. bad" is the natural way it feels to be human. We experience life by qualifying events and assigning values, so it seems very unnatural to use the obverse principle, that there's no right or wrong, there is no good or bad, and there should be no desire for any outcome.

Because in that situation, the energy and time spent by the universe to develop human agency would be wasted. Even a rock can just sit around and not desire to change anything; ants can change things based on instinct alone. So, the concept of consciously changing your environment is predicated upon a desired outcome.

This means there has to be desired and undesired. Good and bad. And we are here to make those calls.

Is God Knowable?

I am not convinced there is a God, and I wrote this to help myself. But could it help someone who does believe? I think it could. Because at the very root of all this stuff, my goal was to make it easier to be comfortable with the unknown. And even those who believe in God share the human experience of not knowing everything.

At the highest level, there are two possible belief structures to explain our universe. One is that God (or some entity that has the attributes of a god, like omnipotent aliens or a really good computer programmer) made a decision to somehow create the Big Bang. Throughout the history of our universe, its guiding hand either helped steer development, or it was all programmed before the Big Bang even banged. And since that decision to Bang the universe, it hasn't really touched anything. Just let the program run. Just like when a computer programmer writes software, the computer can run it without the programmer's input. You don't need a programmer to help you use

Photoshop or Excel. Their work was done before you even started up the program.

The second explanation is that nobody decided our universe should exist; it just sprang forth. It was a purely *natural* phenomenon. This means something natural would have had to occur to create the universe, which means something would have needed to exist in some format before the universe, in some dimension. Which would mean there is no ground zero and no zero hour. Infinite pasts are possible before the universe was created, and we currently have no way of knowing anything about that. Although it's fun to make wild guesses.

In my youth, I had an egotistical tendency to look at people who believe in God the same way I'd look at a teenager who still believes in Santa Claus, with a mixture of disbelief and pity. But what I have come to understand is many of those people are happier than those of us who don't believe in God. Because without God, there can be infinite uncertainty. Not to mention, churches provide tremendous benefits of community and feelings of belonging.

Regardless, what I'm talking about in this book is applicable to both of these worldviews. If you believe in God, then the Root Meaning of being part of the universe would actually be below another super-meaning of being a part of "something created by God." But I'm pretty confident that if you believe in God, you already know how to find meaning through your beliefs.

What physically caused the Big Bang is probably answerable.

"Why did it happen?" may not be, at least through traditional scientific methods.

Was it set into motion by an agent, or did time and space just emerge out of nothing, with no agenda, without anyone deciding to create it? If so, has it happened before? How many universes just pop into existence, and how often?

There may never be a fulfilling answer to this—maybe it's *the* unsolvable problem. There are plenty of scientists who believe that the one true thing about the universe is that it is knowable. Boy, that would be reassuring if true. But that's faith. If you choose to believe it, that makes all of this a lot easier. Because then you can say, "Why does anything exist? Well, that's a hard problem, and I'm going to think about it. Because I know what I'm doing is going to help make progress toward an inevitable answer."

On the other hand, if you come to the conclusion that it's possible to not understand certain things (like why we're here), and there may not be a scientifically *true* answer to that question, then it becomes harder to even think about it because it feels like pointlessly spinning your wheels.

The *unknown* unknown is easy. You just don't know that you don't know it. And you can't worry about something you don't even know about. If all of our internet celebs are actually aliens planning to take over the world, we can't really worry about that, because nobody here expects it. But what if you know for sure that a pirate buried treasure in your neighborhood, but you just don't know exactly where? If you *know* that you *don't know* something, there's a good chance that you will try to keep solving that forever. Especially if you're me.

For a long time, everyone knew for certain

that the sun rotated around the Earth. It was obviously true to everyone, especially scientists of their time. So, maybe there's a way to reconcile the surety of whether or not we will ever know an absolute truth about why we're here, versus the scientific concept of "this is the best answer we have for that question right now."

But if the question is "Why did the universe begin?", how do you form hypotheses around that? How do you test something so seemingly ephemeral? If there turns out to be an elegant equation that marries all four of the known forces (gravity, electromagnetism, strong and weak nuclear), it could be seen as proof of a divine creator by some true believers. It may even convert some skeptical agnostics. But for me, it would only further prove what I already know: the universe is beautiful and intricately interconnected. It doesn't prove authorship.

It becomes hard to find meaning here. I get bogged down because these things are not readily observable or even theorizable.

So instead, I focus on finding meaning where I can find it, not where I can't. The impetus for Creation may be unanswerable.

God may or may not live inside you, but the universe most definitely does. The universe is within your cells and particles and in everything you see: traffic lights, Christmas trees, cold-brew coffee, and dirty windows. We're all made of the same stuff. We've built a really fantastic world around us from all these little things. I choose to enjoy it even though I don't know if it is art or nature.

§

In summary: You are the universe's sense organs, its conscious mind to discover and understand itself, and its ability to decide. No other known entity in the universe can purposefully guide its own evolution. Our specialty is making choices.

You were built to do these specific things. They constitute your purpose for living. You can find a deep meaning in exercising these abilities.

1. **You are the universe.**
2. **Do what you were made to do.**
3. **Deciding is your superpower.**

Root Meaning then is the understanding of all of this. Victor Frankl calls it "super meaning." From his perspective, super meaning is above all else. From mine, it's below. Beneath the meaning you may find by living a life dedicated to your family or to your work, there's a meaning deeper than that. And the deeper meaning allows you to more fully enjoy all those other ways of finding meaning. Understanding root meaning has potential to help folks who may feel at some point that their life is meaningless. That being said, it's not something you need to think about every day. A reminder once a week is plenty. You have things to do, right?

Without a deep foundation of meaning based on understanding our role in the universe, the other meanings we find in life may not seem to serve any larger purpose. That doesn't make them meaningless, but it allows for the possibility.

Just as individuals work for humanity, humanity works for the universe. The next section explores how we do that individually and together.

HUMAN MEANINGS

Humans find meaning by living a purposeful life among other humans. If that sentence isn't an ouroboros, I don't know what is. To better define Human Meaning, it's best to split it up into two big categories.

The first is *Self-Development*, when a person learns to be themself, and grows toward becoming the best version of themself.

The second is *Public Development*, when a person uses their unique talent and perspective to help the rest of the world.

These two activities combine to create a wonderfully meaningful experience. They intertwine and build upon each other. They may happen at different times in your life as phases. For example, going to school is mostly Self-Development, and working for—or creating—a company is mostly Public Development. Often though, Self- and Public Development intertwine and nurture one another in a sort of upward spiral of progress.

Not to beat a dead horse (disgusting habit), but it's much more difficult to find meaning alone than with others. Changing yourself isn't inherently valuable unless it feeds back into a system. There's just no example in nature of one thing by itself. Everything is related to everything else: literally, molecularly, even gravitationally. So, the natural state of being human is to affect other people and affect other things.

§

The life of Siddhartha Gautama (the Buddha) is the story of one man's spiritual journey to enlightenment. It's also the story of what he chose to do after becoming enlightened:

"Although born a prince, Siddhartha Gautama realized that comfortable experiences could not provide lasting happiness or protection from suffering. After a long spiritual search, he went into deep meditation under a bodhi tree, where he realized the nature of mind. He achieved the state of unconditional and lasting happiness: the state of enlightenment, of nirvana. This state of mind is free from disturbing emotions and expresses itself through fearlessness, joy and active compassion.

After his enlightenment, Buddha traveled on foot throughout northern India. He taught constantly for forty-five years. People of all castes and professions, from kings to courtesans, were drawn to him. He answered their questions, always pointing towards that which is ultimately real."

Diamondway Buddhism—"Who Was Buddha?"

Rather than sitting under his tree enjoying this newfound enlightenment for the rest of his life, the Buddha taught anyone who asked how they could reach the same state. He knew that meaning is found by sharing your gifts back to others.

MEANING FOUR:

Become the best you.

Self-Development is directing your own
evolution to nurture unique abilities.

"To be what we are, and to become
what we are capable of becoming, is
the only end of life."

—Robert Louis Stevenson, *Familiar Studies
of Men and Books*

A wonderfully simple answer to the
question "Why am I here?" is that you add
another perspective to the world. As any
successful problem solver will tell you, having
many perspectives is better than one. Seeing
problems from multiple angles and through
multiple lenses allows you to fully understand
the problem. You can solve many problems just
by changing your perspective. Biologically,
over time, having many variations is more
successful than having a few. The value of
human life is not an arbitrary thing. There are
concrete reasons why we should protect and
nurture each person.

**Billions of unique perspectives are
humanity's greatest resource.** They allow us to

see and solve problems from multiple angles, picking the best solution only after finding many options from many paths. A mix of perspectives hedges against short-sighted or uncreative leadership and fights inertia.

So, it's important to protect and enhance diversity. That word, *diversity*, gets used so often that it's important to clarify what I mean in this context: *Genetic* diversity hedges against disease, which can sweep in and wipe out a monoculture in one fell swoop. Nature abhors monocultures. But more important in this context is to protect *perspective* diversity. When everyone is agreeing with everyone else, something is probably wrong. Conflict fuels progress.

So, on an individual level, what does this mean?

First, just be yourself.

Who you are and what you are is already good enough. You are unique. You need only share your perspective with the rest of us based on your own observations and understandings.

Secondly, go deep into what makes you unique and exploit that.

I'm using *exploit* here in the positive sense of discovering and maximizing your potential. You owe it to yourself and to the rest of us to truly develop your own ideas about the world. Don't just consume and regurgitate sound bites and headlines. Modern media makes money by funneling stories into your face that are designed to generate emotion. Instead of forfeiting your mind to them for zero dollars, seek out stories and ideas that are meaningful to you. Think about them and talk about them. Think for yourself based on your own principles. If you don't know what your principles are, think about those first.

Your duty to yourself, human society, and the universe is to swim against the current. Why else would you have such capabilities? Think for yourself and swim upstream. Or hurtle down the waterfall on the comfortable raft of compliance.

To be clear, though, I think it's fine to float downstream sometimes. If you live strictly by your own principles, never giving in to societal pressure or cultural trends, you may have a hard time getting along with your neighbors. The key here, as with all things in life, is finding a good balance. Even iconoclasts wear pants.

Be Your Best Self

For years I struggled with reconciling the notion of *being* versus *doing*. Isn't it enough to just be yourself in your current shape and condition? Why do I need to improve myself or get better?

My answer was simply this: **You change yourself because change is natural. Everything is always changing.**

Change is inevitable and constant, so I'm bound to change over time. I also know that I have the power of agency and can decide how to change things. And I know there are good and bad outcomes, not just an ambiguous, unintentional future. So, with all that in mind, it makes sense to nurture my own growth into a better version of myself, instead of leaving my changes to chance.

So, how do I do that?

Without getting too preachy about how to

be a better person, here are some basic ways I think about growing.

1. Explore. Use your senses to explore the world around you. Get out into the natural world and touch a tree. Touch the soil. Even in our modern, technologically advanced society, nature can teach us so much about existence. Now more than ever before, nature is an important teacher. The cycles of life play out against the background of physical existence. In observing nature, we find similarities that connect to our own work and relationships.

2. Learn. You have the unabridged version of the knowledge of civilization at your fingertips. Use it for something other than Facebooking about the president and posting food photos (guilty of both). Look up something weird that only you care about. (There are at least a hundred people on the internet who love it too.) Go deep and go broad. How much do you know about the Scots Herring Lassies strike of East Anglia in 1938? Do you know how to grow a world-record carrot? Media algorithms will not surface this kind of information. You have to

seek it out.

3.   Practice. Whatever comes to mind when you think, *If I had more time, I'd love to work on X,* that is what you should spend time on. Not all of your time, but some of it. Everyone can find ten minutes during a week. There are 10,080 total, so practicing for 0.09 percent of it is not ideal, but it's a good first step. Get great at things you are good at, and get good at things you're decent at. Wouldn't you like to be twice as good at whatever you love to do? If you improve 1 percent every week, you'll double your ability in seventy weeks ($1.01^{70} = 2$). If you don't practice you'll stay the same ($1.00^{70} = 1$). This assumes exponential rather than linear growth, since I assume you'll get better at practicing each week too.

4.   Enjoy. Savor the tastes, admire the views, smell the smells. Enjoyment does two positive things at once. It lets you relax and recharge. If you're enjoying something, it gives you energy. Some people call this the "Vacation Mindset," where you change your mental state to switch from production mode to restoration

mode. You need to make time to sit under the tree like Buddha. For you, that may mean playing golf or talking to your friend about the meaning of life or drinking a beer. Whatever it might be, that stuff is important. And it's part of the balance. It's part of that pendulum that swings between self and society. The trick here is to learn to enjoy all aspects of life, even the bad ones. Can you learn to enjoy a traffic jam? The point is, it's best to do all this enjoying while you are doing everything else, instead of dedicating small amounts of time for enjoyment. That said, you have to rest. Your body and mind need a break from all of this growth. Bodybuilders know this well. Muscle fiber is only rebuilt during sleep. Get rest, be rested.

Through these four basic ideas, you can create a really positive loop of work and rest that spirals upward. Done together, in sequence and continuously, these methods help you discover and develop your unique gifts.

Remember, you have agency. You can produce change by design, on purpose. Steven Covey says, "You are the programmer, now write your own program." Figure out a plan to build the super-version of yourself.

I always liked the phrase, "The buck stops here," even though I had no idea where it originated. It just sounded like a really powerful and important way to claim responsibility for something. Turns out it came from an old poker phrase. The buck was a marker that was placed in front of the player whose turn it was to deal. Harry Truman said, "The buck stops here," meaning the responsibility was his to take on. I love it even more now. Don't pass the buck when it comes to your own life. The buck stops and starts inside your own skull.

Once you have a game plan, it's up to you to use it. *Just Execute Your Plan*, says the NIKE T-shirt, if I remember correctly. It's your job to make your life better. You do that by considering your own talents and happiness and working to grow them both. No one is coming for you in a helicopter to extract you out of your current situation and fly you to a new, better life.

Except sometimes, they are. The greatest benefit of being a human is that we can rely on other humans for help. You may recall that humans are the most talented and amazing creatures in the known universe. And you have 7.5 billion of them on your team. We'll meet them all in the next chapter.

MEANING FIVE:

Share your gifts.

Public Development is sharing yourself and your abilities with the world to find deeper meaning.

There's this quote, it was attributed to an unknown monk, and it circulated around Tumblr probably fifteen years ago. Someone said it was engraved on the tombstone of an Anglican bishop buried in Westminster Abbey in AD 1100. Knowing the internet, it was probably written by someone who wasn't a monk, somewhere other than Westminster Abbey, and it was probably written in the 1980s. But I don't really care about its origin. The quote is great and meaningful to me:

```
"When I was a young man, I wanted
to change the world.
   I found it was difficult to change
the world, so I tried to change my
nation.
   When I found I couldn't change the
nation, I began to focus on my town. I
couldn't change the town, and as an
older man, I tried to change my
family.
```

Now, as an old man, I realize the only thing I can change is myself, and suddenly I realize that if long ago I had changed myself, I could have made an impact on my family.

My family and I could have made an impact on our town.

Their impact could have changed the nation, and I could indeed have changed the world."

— Found on Tumblr in 2007, supposedly written by an unknown monk around AD 1100

For me, it says that by living a good life and focusing on your smallest "circle of influence" as Steven Covey calls it, you are, in effect, helping the larger system. You don't have to set out to change the world; by improving yourself and your closest relationships, you accomplish that change.

If you step back from that, you start to see that each person is involved in the functioning of human society, a relatively new construction (just a few thousand years old).

My little girl sometimes spends hours making a gift my wife and I. She loves every moment of cutting paper or gluing things or painting. She's immersed in the act of creation, but in the back of her mind she is thinking, *They're going to love this.* We could all benefit from occasionally thinking about what we're doing, and asking, "Who is going to love this?" Feeling that connection and team mentality. This is why alien-invasion stories are so compelling—because we see ourselves from an outside perspective and realize we're all together here as Earthlings.

Here in the U.S. of A., you are relatively free. You can pursue your own happiness, whatever that means for you. For many of us, that means getting money and stuff. Most of us know that we don't really want money and stuff. But we pursue it anyway. The story we are told is that those things bring meaning. That's why ads don't just show a product and explain what it does. They show how the product will give your life more meaning. The car commercial shows a happy family on a road trip, enjoying their life together. The jewelry commercial shows a happy couple giving each other anniversary gifts, celebrating their commitment to each other.

But we all know that money and things alone do not provide meaning. What money actually brings is the opportunity to focus on meaningful things. When you don't have to worry about money, and have enough to pay your bills, you can focus on the things that actually matter. But that means you need to figure out what matters.

So, what *does* actually matter?

Think of a time when you were happiest. Maybe it's your wedding day. Maybe the day your child was born. Maybe the day you got a great job. Aside from happening to you, what do all of these things have in common? Other people.

To contribute to human society, you don't have to do some grand public-works project. Remember the unknown monk. What can you do to start small?

Once you believe that humans are here to perceive, understand, and create, then your role could be defined by it. You could find meaning as a parent or an entrepreneur, or any role in life. You can find deep meaning through helping to increase understanding by studying and solving a problem or helping create more brain power (to further human understanding) by raising and educating a child, or keeping people safe from fire (to maintain more unique valuable perspectives and potentials).

—

I just saw a woman who looked pretty down on her luck walking from a homeless encampment in a nearby park. She had a plastic grocery bag in one hand and protectively held a half-eaten donut in the other as she was haphazardly crossing the middle of the street at noon on a Monday. As I watched her, I had this immediate brief moment where I put myself in her place. I thought, maybe, when she got that donut, she thought, *This is going to be some good energy for me, some good fuel. Good energy for me right now.*

Just that little thought *I* had about *her* thoughts made me realize how quickly and easily you can put yourself into someone else's perspective. What a valuable and distinctly human skill that is. It speaks to the fact that we are all pieces of the same whole. The illusion that things are separate is stubbornly persistent. Because we are all related (on average, seventh cousins), we're all physically connected, and we're all made of the same stuff.

Regardless of what they're doing in life, everyone is trying to positively affect others. Even the most ostentatious displays of unearned wealth are rooted in some desire for good. The #yachtlife guy coasting on his inheritance is, deep down, probably sabering that champagne bottle because he wants his dad to feel pride or his girlfriend to feel like she picked a good provider. The travel influencer displaying her butt on the edge of some mountain lagoon must believe that she is inspiring others to "dream big" or something like that. They are trying to "do something good" in their own minds. The problem is that many people have the wrong idea about what is good. Many people waste their unique abilities and do things for money or prestige, rather than from a desire to do their best work.

But whether you're a welder fixing a bridge to keep people safe, an advertising copywriter trying to make people laugh, or a mother trying to raise her children and improve upon how she was raised (which happens in every generation), all of those things are directly related to other people. Even people with demonstrably bad ideas about how society should be organized are usually promoting those ideas from a place of helpfulness.

> "No man really knows about other human beings. The best he can do is to suppose that they are like himself."
>
> —John Steinbeck, *The Winter of Our Discontent*

It's not surprising that the more you help other people, the happier you are. "Studies show" that to be true. Interestingly, helping others also improves our feeling of autonomy and agency. It helps us remember that we can freely choose our own actions, and that we are good, capable humans. And helping others, obviously, makes us feel close to our fellow humans.

That feeling of connection is incredibly powerful. Remember that you are part of a vast, mind-bogglingly connected system. A single cell in my body exerts a force on a star on the other side of the galaxy. Gravity does not have a distance limit. If you put two molecules of hydrogen a billion light years apart, those two molecules would be attracted to each other. It is immeasurably small, but it is greater than zero. For me, this surprising scientific truth contributes as much to the meaning of life as it does to physics. Literally everything in the universe is connected in this way.

That thought experiment about the value of a solitary human is null and void, because there cannot be a single anything. Each individual thread is part of the fabric.

So, what can the individual do to find meaning in such a complex system?

From the point of view of the universe, a person's goal should be to improve human society, because humanity is the universe's best chance at understanding and changing itself. And the best way to do that is not to think about yourself as the most important thing in the world. It's to think about how you fit into the most important thing in the world, human society.

A human could not build the Brooklyn Bridge, but human society can. A human couldn't travel to space, but human society can. A human couldn't colonize the galaxy, but human society can. The success of human society is the success of the universe.

But here's the rub. That can become a really frustrating loop. Am I just here to help other people, and are they here to help other people, so that those people can help other people? What's the point of that? Why are we all just helping each other all the time?

What about me? Am I just a neuron in the global brain? Just one little thinking node in the functioning network? And I just have to try to help my little neighboring neurons fire better so that we can all function smoothly. I need to be a successful cog!

It's a little bit devastating when you picture it that way. Because if we get too far down that path, then you have people sacrificing their own goodness and well-being for the sake of other people, which is counterproductive. State-run socialism and communism have failed to become as successful as capitalism partly because of this flaw. So, the point I'm trying to make isn't that you should go out and sacrifice yourself all the time for other people or causes. The point is that your drive inside—why you're doing things—ought to be related to helping us all grow together. Your work, your most important contributions, ought to provide some value to society.

The problems we face feel so individually unique. We're taught from an early age that we are unique. And the truth is, we are! But that makes it hard to live our lives continually thinking about our place in a larger system.

Without wading into our broken political system, it's fair to say that there are pros and cons to all systems of government. Might we combine the best concepts of libertarian capitalism, collectivist socialism, and consolidated monarchy into something that can work better for us right now? Not forever, but right now? We don't have to create a forever system. That's the great thing about human society. We move quick. Sometimes too quick. But with increasing speed, we may be just a few short societal evolutions away from utopia! (Kidding.)

Some of us talk about freedom, independence, and the pursuit of happiness.

Some of us talk about connection,

interdependence, and the pursuit of a unified society.

In the *combined* pursuit of these ideas, we create a better future for ourselves and others.

SUMMARY OF
HUMAN MEANING

The Loop

As you learn and grow, you expand your capacity for change. This wonderful concept is called exponential growth.

As your capacity grows larger, you possess more ability to change the world. That includes the world inside your skin, as well as outside. The amazing looping nature of human growth is that the more you grow, the more you can grow. That's why it's so important to start growing as early as possible. It's why we focus so much energy (but not enough) on childhood education. It's like a retirement investment account. The earlier you start, the more time your money has to build interest, which, in turn, accrues interest.

The universe is doing the same thing, by the way. As it expands and grows, it does so faster and faster. Instead of slowing down, it is actually speeding up as it expands. Nobody is sure why this is happening, only that it is. My completely uneducated guess is that some field or particle is building up exponentially. It fit my narrative, anyway.

As you build yourself up through self-development, you can find meaning by changing the world through public development. The looping nature of this process means that sometimes they overlap, and other times you may spend years doing one so that you can better do the other.

Think about how many years of education we go through in our youth, and why we do that. We believe it's important to develop ourselves into productive members of society, so we can go out and help the cause. Sometimes this period of education lasts well into our twenties. That's one quarter of your life dedicated to building yourself up and self-development, before you're even asked to help change the world through public development. For some "eternal student" types, the time never seems to come. For reasons known only to them, they never want to step out into the real world and share their gifts.

For others, the loop may be a year or so of intense training before they are able to share their new skill with the public. My friend Josh Smith runs an excellent metal shop called Clutch Fabrication. He teaches young people how to cut and weld, and their apprenticeship usually takes a year or so. In the past, apprentices would pay a tradesman to learn by their side for up to seven years. Now there are fewer young people interested in learning a trade, and the tradesman almost always pays the apprentice for their time. After a year, the apprentice has enough skill to complete projects by himself. At that point, they either work for the tradesman for a couple more years, or they go out and get a job from a contractor or manufacturer. Then the loop starts over again.

In other situations, the loop may be even shorter. Think about how quickly a new mom has to adjust to being a parent. They may have read all the books about it, but once that baby comes, the education really begins. A tornado of new challenges rumbles through the home every single day, and they quickly learn how to handle them all. They develop the skills needed to care for a newborn and quickly use those skills to help the child survive and thrive. The loop lasts less than a day, usually less than an hour. When a baby is crying, you figure out how to stop it, and you do that thing *now*.

Starting a business is similarly intense. You

may have a business degree and read all the right blogs and listen to all the right podcasts. But nothing can teach you to run a business, aside from actually doing it. You are forced to learn something new every day and use that learning immediately to solve the problem. The fun part is that starting a business is very different from running it. Starting a business is like a sprint against a beast called inertia. Your job is to overcome tremendous resistance and bring something brand new into existence. All the while, the inertia beast is throwing hurdles down in your path. Need a building? Here's a hundred-page building code and lease negotiation. Need a license? Here's the industry code book and fifty-page application. Need money? Here's a hundred people and banks who will tell you no before you find the one who says yes.

Then, once you open for business, you cross the finish line, only to find that your sprint was the starting leg of a marathon for your life against a bunch of competitive gazelles that never ends.

$\S$

This loop concept is an incredibly useful tool for me. When I'm having a hard time, or just not feeling like my work is coming out right, I try to remember what my son's pediatrician told me.

My son is a picky eater. He didn't used to be that way, and evidently, he will grow out of it. In the meantime, I was concerned about the sheer volume of pasta he was eating. "Doctor, will my son turn into a noodle?" We try to put a variety of foods in front of him every meal, but he whines if he doesn't get noodles.

She said not to worry about variety for every meal, but to try to make sure he gets variety every week. Let him eat as much spaghetti as he wants for a couple of meals, or even a couple of days. Eventually he's going to crave the fruit or the carrots, because his body is telling him he needs those things.

In the same way, you don't need to be contributing back to society every minute of every day. You will burn out really quickly if you try to do that. Instead, realize that you can spend time recharging your batteries. Do things that help you recharge, because you're going to need that energy to change the world.

You're clack-clack-clacking your way up the roller coaster hill, and on the other side, you get to throw your hands up and scream.

And you'll go through phases. You'll spend a large percentage of your younger years just learning and developing yourself. You'll find your talents. You'll learn to enjoy life in the ways you find most fulfilling.

Then hopefully in your middle years, you'll be able to bring something back to the group. You'll probably work too much during this time, giving too much of yourself, as so many people do.

But then in your later years, you may be able to find a balance. You'll make time for yourself and time for contributing back on a daily basis. It may take a lifetime to develop that ability.

The Meaning of Love

I need to explain something before I go too much further. Some people will be thinking around now, "What about love? What about your family? Can't you be happy with being loved and having a loving family? How can you write a book about the meaning of life and not focus on love?"

The amount of positive energy I get by spending time with my family is immeasurable. Young children have a gleam in their eyes that hasn't been dulled by life's struggles. They have infinite optimism and creativity, without the boundaries of tradition. I learn more from talking to my six-year-old boy and four-year-old girl than I could possibly glean from hours of watching or reading the news.

So, my family is at the top of my list. But the list has other things on it. And the other things are important too. Creating. Building. Contributing back to society. Doing valuable work. Receiving some recognition of its value (either money or gratitude). These things sit on the same list as intimacy, love, and family, and sometimes overtake them. Especially during the working hours of the week. My priority changes based on time and space.

I sometimes wish that weren't the case, and maybe it will change as I grow older. For now, I'm being honest with you, myself, my family. Work is important. Work is meaningful. By doing meaningful work, I am a whole person. And being a whole person means I can better love my family.

I know this book is pretty hard-nosed and logical. I have that tendency. I have a hard nose. In the heat of an argument, as I stand there with my arms at my side, not yelling, not showing any outward signs of emotion, I have heard, "Can you please tell me how you're feeling, robot?" And that is a fair volley to throw my way during a fight. But this robot does have human emotions (got an upgrade chip a while back).

Likewise, you can get by on love and enjoyment alone too. Some folks just don't want to be bothered with all of this reasoning. I know a lot of people like this, and they live very happy lives. Good for them. They wouldn't be reading this book anyway, so we can make fun of them now. Look at how happy and unconcerned with questing for meaning they are. Look at how happy they are. Ha ha, wow, they are happy. Damn.

$\int$

"Well, I've wrestled with reality for thirty-five years, Doctor, and I'm happy to state I finally won out over it."

—Mary Chase, Harvey

For most people, there is a balance between searching for meaning, and enjoying love and life. This is as it should be.

Love is what really binds all of this book's logical and tactical ideas together. You can get by on reason and logic alone, and I occasionally have. But without love, you won't experience the deepest feelings of meaningfulness. Love can elevate all of these logical ideas to the status of perfect meaning.

Here are a few ways I think about love as the binding agent of human meaning.

A Love List

- Appreciate the incredible position we find ourselves in, individually, and as a species.
- Show tenderness for your fellow

travelers (partner, family, friends, neighbors, animals).

- Devote yourself to your purpose. Devotion is a powerful form of love.
- Compare your woes with the immensity of the universe, and this new perspective may help reframe yourself and your life.
- Cultivate passion and infatuation with small pieces of the world: your unique areas of focus (maybe a person, maybe a niche field of interest).
- Embrace your personal style and tastes.
- Appreciate sublime moments of poignancy in film, music, visual art, and theater.
- Delight when you discover something new, create something wonderful, or share something with the world.

CONCLUSION
Finding meaning through purpose

A lot of what we read and hear today are messages of despair. Most media companies continuously broadcast various forms of "the end is near" because fear sells. The oceans are rising. The plants and animals are all dying. Everyone hates everyone else.

That does not inspire solutions. It just makes media companies money, and the rest of us miserable.

When a problem presents itself in our daily lives, at home or at work, we don't sit in a corner with our head in our hands. We don't talk about the problem without also talking about possible solutions.

Yelling that "the ship is sinking" is useful, but only until everyone on board is aware of the problem. After that, the yelling needs to stop, and the work needs to begin.

We need to be honest and see reality for what it is, warts and all. But we also need a vision for a better future. People want to fix a sinking ship. We should say, "The ship is sinking. We need to stay afloat so that we can keep sailing and get to this promised land," and keep reminding ourselves of what good things may lie ahead.

For now, that promised land is unclear. And if we don't have a shared positive vision for the future, it's difficult to get people to fix the ship.

The hardest problems we face are not the ones that get the most media attention (environment, politics, economy). Those are the symptoms, not the disease. The problem is that we don't have a vision for our future that we can all rally behind. Without a strategy, we will never be able to solve the tactical problems of how best to organize our society and shepherd our planet.

Sometimes these global-scale problems we face seem so complex that it feels pointless to even try to wrap your head around them. But compared to trying to figure out the meaning of life, our ecological and economic problems all seem to be solvable. Not easy, but not impossible. At the center of it is love and open communication. That seems like a big stretch for America right now, but we have it in us. Baby steps.

S

Meaningful Futures

"So why try to predict the future
at all if it's so difficult, so nearly
impossible? Because making predictions
is one way to give warning when we see
ourselves drifting in dangerous
directions. Because prediction is a
useful way of pointing out safer,
wiser courses. **Because, most of all,
our tomorrow is the child of our
today.** Through thought and deed, we
exert a great deal of influence over
this child, even though we can't
control it absolutely. Best to think
about it, though. Best to try to shape
it into something good. Best to do
that for any child."

—Octavia Butler

Having a future is essential for finding
meaning in life. Not knowing if you have
"something to live for" results in a meaningless
existence. So meaning is directly related to the
future. And here is where it gets difficult
because we can't know the future.

But we do know that it will likely be better than the present. Maybe not next year, maybe not even next decade. But the future is bright for humanity, and we can prove this with a handy bit of thinking from Viktor Frankl.

"The question was whether an ape which was being used to develop a poliomyelitis vaccine, and for this reason punctured again and again, would ever be able to grasp the meaning of its suffering. Unanimously, the group replied that of course it would not; with its limited intelligence, it could not enter into the world of man, i.e., the only world in which the meaning of its suffering would be understandable.

Then I pushed forward with the following question: 'And what about man? Are you sure that the human world is a terminal point in the evolution of the cosmos? Is it not conceivable that there is still another dimension, a world beyond man's world; a world in which the question of an ultimate meaning of human suffering would find an answer?'"

—*Victor Frankl, Man's Search for Meaning*

The ape is subjected to injections in order to find a cure for a disease. The ape doesn't have the capacity to understand that its sacrifice is beneficial to others. Similarly, current human consciousness is not able to understand the meaning of life as thoroughly as a future version of us might. So, it's worth working toward that. It's worth doing what we can to direct our own evolution toward it. Call it meaning-focused self-directed evolution; let's work on things that help us understand ourselves in the context of the universe.

We are not the destination, just a milestone in the evolution of consciousness.

But we're alive right now! Our meaning happens now! So, we can find meaning in our daily lives by knowing that we serve the purpose of getting us all closer to a more ideal reality. *Striving for ideal* is not the same as *idealism*. You can pragmatically aim for perfection, knowing you'll never achieve it. Through that process, you will continually improve.

What would humanity look like in an ideal future? Bigger brains, smaller bodies probably. Maybe some cool antennae. But that's not what I'm asking. What would human society and conscious life look like?

I can't answer that for you. It's up to each of us to guide our own conscious evolution toward the things that we value. Do you want to become more analytical and algorithmic in our thinking? Do you want to become more sensitive to other people's emotions or needs? Do you want a greater ability to communicate directly with other people, or possibly nonhuman life? Do you want to leave this planet and colonize others, beginning new lines of human evolution? Do you want to further integrate with machines so that you can change and control your environment at larger scales? We can each direct our evolution toward our own ideal futures. In some instances, we have the ability to use genetic manipulation and brain manipulation to speed up that evolution.

Diversity of perspective requires a lot of different visions and goals. And one of them doesn't necessarily have to "win," either.

Multiple evolutions of humanity are possible at once.

Tying Everything Together

The strange loop of the meaning of life is this: in order for the universe to understand and change itself, it had to create humans. In order to be good humans, we have to find meaning. In order to find meaning, we have to realize we are the universe.

The universe is constantly expanding and reforming itself. Our galaxy and solar system are part of that, and our planet is part of that. And on Earth, which seems to be a rare, habitable version of a planet, life has taken over. Over a few billion years, living things have colonized nearly every surface, nook, cranny, and drop of water. And fairly recently, for some reason, life spent a great deal of energy to create smart animals who can ask why we are here.

We can observe each other, the rest of the world, and the cosmos. And we are conscious of our own consciousness—we are aware that we are aware. This actually causes some problems for us. Turns out it's difficult to be fully aware of what's happening right now, when we are simultaneously aware of that awareness and trying to assign some kind of meaning to it. It's a messy business, and our brain has to do a lot of work to keep things straight. The ultimate multitasking is living life while trying to understand why you're alive.

But consciousness is also a great gift because we can plan ahead and solve complicated problems like figuring out the meaning of life. Or at least we can try.

So, we are the universe observing itself, through a level of consciousness that may never have existed before. Our brains are the most complex things in the universe, as far as we know. We're walking around balancing them up on top of these big bags of meat and blood and bone, mostly unaware of how incredibly powerful they are. The cause of—and solution to—all of life's greatest problems is the human brain.

§

Root Meaning is found from thinking big picture. It answers the questions, "What is the point of humanity existing in the first place?" and "Why are we here and trying to find meaning and purpose?" This is the intellectual part of meaning. It is the logical root system that supports all the other things you do. The reason humanity exists is to provide the universe with a set of sense organs and an analytical mind to discover, understand, and change itself. And as humans, we have the capacity to change the universe to suit our own purpose (which is inherently also the universe's purpose, since we're the universe).

Human Meaning is related to how, on a day-to-day basis, we're improving our own lot in life, decreasing suffering, increasing understanding, finding joy, helping others, contributing something back to the group. The much simpler way of saying this one is: work hard and help others. You will not be able to find deep meaning without that key ingredient.

The path to finding a deeper meaning in life is littered with the skins you shed through finding your purpose.

§

Remember that you're never alone in this world. We are many, and compassion comes easy to us. For every news story about something terrible, there are a million kind interactions between strangers that go unreported. We rely on each other and trust each other. When a motorist is stranded on the side of the highway, more people offer help than is ever needed. When bridges are built, the foreman doesn't need to check every weld. He knows that the welder will consider the safety of his fellow humans and take his work seriously.

Here's one of my favorite stories about trust, and I remember it every time I'm driving in the dark.

"One night recently, I was driving down a two-lane highway at about 60 miles an hour. A car approached from the opposite direction at about the same speed. As we passed each other, I caught the other driver's eye for only a second.

I wondered whether he might be thinking, as I was, how dependent we were on each other at that moment. I was relying on him not to fall asleep, not to be distracted by a cell phone conversation, not to cross over into my lane and bring my life suddenly to an end. And though we had never spoken a word to one another, he relied upon me in just the same way.

Multiplied a million times over, I believe that is the way the world works. At some level, we all depend upon one another. Sometimes that dependence requires us simply to refrain from doing something like crossing over the double yellow line. And sometimes it requires us to act cooperatively, with allies or even with strangers."

—Warren Christopher, *This I Believe*

Not only do we depend on each other for our lives and for our pursuits, we depend on each other for meaning. The meaning of life, at human scale, is found by using your unique gifts to the best of your ability and sharing your work with others. There is nothing more satisfying, more loving, and more meaningful that you can do.

The fact that society is only a few thousand years old means our skills of cooperation and interdependence haven't had much time to evolve, especially at global scale. Our basic human skills of observation, understanding, creation and decision are much more refined and powerful.

The answer to how we should organize ourselves for the best chance of success as a species is still unclear. But it should be very obvious that any limitations we artificially place on individual creativity and agency are surely a step down the wrong path.

$$\mathcal{S}$$

You were just handed the keys to the universe. Where are you going to take us? Think as big as you can, and start as small as you can. Explore the edges of possibility. The only difference between most people and the names in your history book is that those people acted on their ideas instead of just thinking about them.

Remember that you are the universe, and the universe is everything.

ABOUT THE AUTHOR

Adam Quirk lives in Unionville, Indiana, USA

adamquirk.com

www.ingramcontent.com/pod-product-compliance
Lightning Source LLC
Chambersburg PA
CBHW070812050426
42452CB00011B/2004